AT THE END OF THE OPEN ROAD

AT
THE
END
OF
THE
OPEN ROAD

POEMS BY *Louis Simpson*

WESLEYAN UNIVERSITY PRESS
Middletown, Connecticut

Certain poems in this book have appeared in the following magazines, and the author acknowledges their permission to reprint: *The Hudson Review, The Paris Review, The Noble Savage, Contact, The Sixties, Metamorphosis, Generation, The New Statesman, The American Scholar, The Quarterly Review, Epoch.* The following poems originally appeared in *The New Yorker:* "The Silent Lover"; "The Sea and the Forest" (originally titled "Sailors"); "My Father in the Night Commanding No"; "A Farm in Minnesota."

The author is grateful to the John Simon Guggenheim Memorial Foundation for a grant which enabled him to finish this book.

Library of Congress Catalog Card Number: 63-17792
Manufactured in the United States of America
First printing, September 1963; second printing, May 1964

For Matthew, Anne, and Anthony

CONTENTS

I

IN CALIFORNIA

Here I am, troubling the dream coast
With my New York face,
Bearing among the realtors
And tennis-players my dark preoccupation.

There once was an epical clatter—
Voices and banjos, Tennessee, Ohio,
Rising like incense in the sight of heaven.
Today, there is an angel in the gate.

Lie back, Walt Whitman,
There, on the fabulous raft with the King and the
        Duke!
For the white row of the Marina
Faces the Rock. Turn round the wagons here.

Lie back! We cannot bear
The stars any more, those infinite spaces.
Let the realtors divide the mountain,
For they have already subdivided the valley.

Rectangular city blocks astonished
Herodotus in Babylon,
Cortez in Tenochtitlan,
And here's the same old city-planner, death.

We cannot turn or stay.
For though we sleep, and let the reins fall slack,
The great cloud-wagons move
Outward still, dreaming of a Pacific.

IN THE SUBURBS

There's no way out.
You were born to waste your life.
You were born to this middleclass life

As others before you
Were born to walk in procession
To the temple, singing.

THE REDWOODS

Mountains are moving, rivers
are hurrying. But we
are still.

We have the thoughts of giants —
clouds, and at night the stars.

And we have names — gutteral, grotesque —
Hamet, Og — names with no syllables.

And perish, one by one, our roots
gnawed by the mice. And fall.

And are too slow for death, and change
to stone. Or else too quick,

like candles in a fire. Giants
are lonely. We have waited long

for someone. By our waiting, surely
there must be someone at whose touch

our boughs would bend; and hands
to gather us; a spirit

to whom we are light as the hawthorn tree.
O if there is a poet

let him come now! We stand at the Pacific
like great unmarried girls,

turning in our heads the stars and clouds,
considering whom to please.

THERE IS

Look! From my window there's a view
of city streets
where only lives as dry as tortoises
can crawl — the Gallapagos of desire.

There is the day of Negroes with red hair
and the day of insane women on the subway;
there is the day of the word Trieste
and the night of the blind man with the electric guitar.

But I have no profession. Like a spy
I read the papers — Situations Wanted.
Surely there is a secret
which, if I knew it, would change everything!

2

I have the poor man's nerve-tic, irony.
I see through the illusions of the age!
The bell tolls, and the hearse advances,
and the mourners follow, for my entertainment.

I tread the burning pavement,
the streets where drunkards stretch
like photographs of civil death
and trumpets strangle in electric shelves.

The mannequins stare at me scornfully.
I know they are pretending
all day to be in earnest.
And can it be that love is an illusion?

When darkness falls on the enormous street
the air is filled with Eros, whispering.
Eyes, mouths, contrive to meet
in silence, fearing they may be prevented.

3

O businessmen like ruins,
bankers who are Bastilles,
widows, sadder than the shores of lakes,
then you were happy, when you still could tremble!

But all night long my window
sheds tears of light.
I seek the word. The word is not forthcoming.
O syllables of light . . . O dark cathedral . . .

II

SUMMER MORNING

There are whole blocks in New York
Where no one lives —
A district of small factories.
And there's a hotel; one morning

When I was there with a girl
We saw in the window opposite
Men and women working at their machines.
Now and then one looked up.

Toys, hardware — whatever they made,
It's been worn out.
I'm fifteen years older myself —
Bad years and good.

So I have spoiled my chances.
For what? Sheer laziness,
The thrill of an assignation,
My life that I hold in secret.

THE SILENT LOVER

She sighs. What shall I say?
For beauty seems to grow
In silence, when the heart is faint and slow.

Sing, sing . . . How shall I sing?
In silent eyes, where clouds and islands gaze,
The waves bring Eros in.

I think the rustling of her clothes
Is like the sea, and she
A wild white bird,

And love is like the sighing of the sand.

BIRCH

Birch tree, you remind me
Of a room filled with breathing,
The sway and whisper of love.

She slips off her shoes;
Unzips her skirt; arms raised,
Unclasps an earring, and the other.

Just so the sallow trunk
Divides, and the branches
Are pale and smooth.

THE SEA AND THE FOREST

A woman appears on deck.

In her shy look the sailors
Inhale the perfume of swamp roots
And certain dark streets of Marseilles.

She stands still in a shadow.

Voices of children rising from the sea,
Air bells and flowers. . . .

Or maybe she is thinking of a house,
One of those little streets in Paris
Where lovers twitter like canaries.

Or maybe it's a forest.
The leaves are hushed and still.

All this, and more, the sailors
Think of while she stands,
One hand lightly resting on the rail.

Farewell, my old pine forest!
I might have lived there for a thousand years.

THE MORNING LIGHT

In the morning light a line
Stretches forever. There my unlived life
Rises, and I resist,
Clinging to the steps of the throne.

Day lifts the darkness from the hills,
A bright blade cuts the reeds,
And my life, pitilessly demanding,
Rises forever in the morning light.

THE CRADLE TRAP

A bell and rattle,
a smell of roses,
a leather Bible,
and angry voices . . .

They say, I love you.
They shout, You must!
The light is telling
terrible stories.

But night at the window
whispers, Never mind.
Be true, be true
to your own strange kind.

A STORY ABOUT CHICKEN SOUP

In my grandmother's house there was always
    chicken soup
And talk of the old country—mud and boards,
Poverty,
The snow falling down the necks of lovers.

Now and then, out of her savings
She sent them a dowry. Imagine
The rice-powdered faces!
And the smell of the bride, like chicken soup.

But the Germans killed them.
I know it's in bad taste to say it,
But it's true. The Germans killed them all.

                    *

In the ruins of Berchtesgaden
A child with yellow hair
Ran out of a doorway.

A German girl-child—
Cuckoo, all skin and bones—
Not even enough to make chicken soup.
She sat by the stream and smiled.

Then as we splashed in the sun
She laughed at us.
We had killed her mechanical brothers,
So we forgave her.

*

The sun is shining.
The shadows of the lovers have disappeared.
They are all eyes; they have some demand on me—
They want me to be more serious than I want to be.

They want me to stick in their mudhole
Where no one is elegant.
They want me to wear old clothes,
They want me to be poor, to sleep in a room
        with many others—

Not to walk in the painted sunshine
To a summer house,
But to live in the tragic world forever.

THE TROIKA

Troika, troika! The snow moon
whirls through the forest.

Where lamplight like a knife
gleams through a door, I see two graybeards bending.
They're playing chess, it seems. And then one rises
and stands in silence. Does he hear me passing?

Troika, troika! In the moonlight
his spirit hears my spirit passing.

I whip the horses on. The houses vanish.
The moon looks over fields
littered with debris. And there in trenches
the guardsmen stand, wind fluttering their rags.

And there were darker fields without a moon.
I walk across a field, bound on an errand.
The errand's forgotten—something depended on it.
A nightmare! I have lost my father's horses!

And then a white bird rises
and goes before me, hopping through the forest.

I held the bird—it vanished with a cry,
and on a branch a girl sat sideways, combing
her long black hair. The dew
shone on her lips; her breasts were white as roses.

Troika, troika! Three white horses,
a whip of silver, and my father's sleigh . . .

When morning breaks, the sea
gleams through the branches,
and the white bird, enchanted,
is flying through the world, across the sea.

NEW LINES FOR CUSCUSCARAWAY
AND MIRZA MURAD ALI BEG

"... the particular verse we are going to get will be cheerful, dry and
sophisticated."

— T. E. HULME

O amiable prospect!
O kingdom of heaven on earth!
I saw Mr. Eliot leaning over a fence
Like a cheerful embalmer,
And two little Indians with black umbrellas
Seeking admission,
And I was rapt in a song
Of *sophist*ication.
O City of God!
Let us be thoroughly dry.
Let us sing a new song unto the Lord,
A song of exclusion.
For it is not so much a matter of being chosen
As of not being excluded.
I will sing unto the Lord
In a voice that is cheerfully dry.

The Prince of Monaco
Was sick of English ladies.

The Prince had a yacht
And her name was *Hirondelle.*
She was cousin to the yacht of the Kaiser
And niece to the yacht of the Tsar.

And the Prince was interested in the sea—
That is, oceanography.
So he furnished the yacht with instruments
And with instruments of brass,
Burners and sinks and instruments
Of the most delicate glass.

There was also a whaleboat
And a whole crew of harpooners.
There was a helmet and suit of armor
For the wars of the ocean floor.

The *Hirondelle* trembled like a fern,
And the crew stood at attention,
And they piped the Captain aboard.

2

Cloud-sailed, the *Hirondelle*
Pursued the horizon.
At night she skimmed
The phosphorescent surges.

And now they are on the Pacific,
The bottomless sea.

And out of the deep they have drawn
The whale, Leviathan, with a hook.
They have captured the giant squid
That has ten arms, claws like a cat's, a beak
     like a parrot's,
And a large malevolent eye.

They stepped from the whaleboat onto shoals,
The crests of sunken mountains.
In nets they gathered
Plankton and weeds and crabs that looked astonished.

And there were nights, O Prince,
When you stretched your hands and feet
In the leaves of the pomegranate tree!

And all went into the log.
The various sea trophies
Were written down in the log.
The darkening sky, the storm,
And tranquil days—
All, all went into the log.

3

The Prince returned—a hero of sorts.
He returned to his former life,
To the lights of the Grand Hotel
And the Russian ladies with their eternal cigarettes.

Then he built a museum.
The wheel of the *Hirondelle* is there,
And also the laboratory, the strange heart of the ship

Uprooted, leaving red holes
In the deck that vanished in smoke.

Here are the trophies:
A walking stick made from the backbone of a shark;
Tortoiseshell combs, and fans of mother-of-pearl;
Corals that faded,
Losing the changing hues of sea and sky;
Sea shells under glass
That are as dull as buttons
Sewn on garments by girls who have faded.

The Philippine Islands are a box
And the smile of a lady in a mantilla.

A walrus stuffed with straw
Faces the diving helmet.
They remember Verdun and Passchendaele,
The mud-clouded wars of the ocean floor.

So all that oceanography, after all,
Was only a pawnshop.
For they brought home the tooth of the whale
And said, "Look!
It is only a doorstop, after all."

For Leviathan does not exist,
And the sea is no mystery.
For a shark is a walking stick.

And this we call the life of reason.

4

Idiots!
We too are all for reducing
The universe to human dimensions.
As if we could know what is human!

Just a few dippers of sea water
And a fair wind home . . .
Then surely we won't be destroyed.

A strange idea, if you consider
The dust of those settlements—
The parlors where no one lives;
The splinter that wounds the foot-sole
On its way to the double bed;
And Leviathan over all,
The cloud shaped like a weasel or a whale,
Leviathan rising above the roof tops.

5

When men wanted the golden fleece
It was not wool they wanted.
They were the trophies that they sailed toward.

They were the sea and the wind
That hurled them over
Into the sea. They were the fishes
That stripped their thin bones. And they rose
In the night in new constellations.

They left no wreckage.
Nothing is floating on the surface.
For they yielded themselves
To the currents that moved from within.

They are mightily changed
In the corollas, the branched sea-heaven.

And you, my country,
These days your walls are moving,
These nights we are branching among the stars.

I say, but my mind is doubtful.
Are there any at sea?
If so, they have not whispered lately.

MARINE—AFTER RIMBAUD

The chariots of silver and copper—
The prows of steel and silver—
Beat the foam—
Tear at the roots of brambles.
The offshore currents,
And the huge paths of the ebbing tide,
Circle toward the east,
Toward the pillars of the forest—
Toward the timbers of the pier
Where it is bending wounded with whirlpools
        of light.

FROGS

The storm broke, and it rained,
And water rose in the pool,
And frogs hopped into the gutter,

With their skins of yellow and green,
And just their eyes shining above the surface
Of the warm solution of slime.

At night, when fireflies trace
Light-lines between the trees and flowers
Exhaling perfume,

The frogs speak to each other
In rhythm. The sound is monstrous,
But their voices are filled with satisfaction.

In the city I pine for the country;
In the country I long for conversation—
Our happy croaking.

MY FATHER IN THE NIGHT COMMANDING NO

My father in the night commanding No
Has work to do. Smoke issues from his lips;
    He reads in silence.
The frogs are croaking and the streetlamps glow.

And then my mother winds the gramophone;
The Bride of Lammermoor begins to shriek—
    Or reads a story
About a prince, a castle, and a dragon.

The moon is glittering above the hill.
I stand before the gateposts of the King—
    So runs the story—
Of Thule, at midnight when the mice are still.

And I have been in Thule! It has come true—
The journey and the danger of the world,
    All that there is
To bear and to enjoy, endure and do.

Landscapes, seascapes ... . where have I been led?
The names of cities—Paris, Venice, Rome—
    Held out their arms.
A feathered god, seductive, went ahead.

Here is my house. Under a red rose tree
A child is swinging; another gravely plays.
    They are not surprised
That I am here; they were expecting me.

And yet my father sits and reads in silence,
My mother sheds a tear, the moon is still,
  And the dark wind
Is murmuring that nothing ever happens.

Beyond his jurisdiction as I move
Do I not prove him wrong? And yet, it's true
  They will not change
There, on the stage of terror and of love.

The actors in that playhouse always sit
In fixed positions—father, mother, child
  With painted eyes.
How sad it is to be a little puppet!

Their heads are wooden. And you once pretended
To understand them! Shake them as you will,
  They cannot speak.
Do what you will, the comedy is ended.

Father, why did you work? Why did you weep,
Mother? Was the story so important?
  "Listen!" the wind
Said to the children, and they fell asleep.

III

THE MARRIAGE OF POCAHONTAS

These episodes are taken
From Captain, sometimes Governor, John Smith's
Generall Historie of Virginia,
New England, and the Summer Isles.

How far he tells the truth,
Seeing that he was baiting hooks
To catch investors,
I leave to the reader's judgment.
This, for example,
From his epistle to a duchess,
To my mind shows a theatrical
Extravagant spirit:

"When I was slave to the Turkes,
The beauteous Lady Tragabigzanda
Did all she could to secure me.
When I overcame the Bashaw of Nalbrits,
The charitable Lady Callamata
Supplyed my necessities.
In the utmost of many necessities,
That blessed Pocahontas,
The great Kings daughter of Virginia,
Oft saved my life."

Lady Tragabigzanda!
Lady Callamata!
Not to mention the Bashaw of Nalbrits!

But we may be too suspicious
In this too timid age.
When the world was expanding, language wore

Big breeches and odd jerkins and strange sleeves.

So then, this is the story
Of Smith's extremities
And King Powhatan and his dearest daughter.

1. *Pocahontas Saves His Life*

At last they brought him to Meronocomo
Where was Powhatan their Emperor.
More than two hundred of those grim courtiers
Stood wondering at him,
As he had been a monster,
Till Powhatan and his train
Had put themselves in their greatest braveries.

Before a fire upon a seat
The King sat covered with a robe
Of rarowcun skins, and all the tails hanging by.
On either side sat a young wench
Of sixteen or eighteen years;
Along each side of the house, two rows of men;
Behind them, as many women,
With all their heads and shoulders painted red;
Many of their heads bedecked
With the white down of birds;
But everyone with something,
And a great chain of beads about their necks.

At his entrance before the King
All the people gave a great shout.
The queen of Appamatuck

Brought him water to wash his hands;
Another, a bunch of feathers to dry them.

Having feasted him after their best barbarous manner,
A long consultation was held,
But the conclusion was
Two great stones were brought before Powhatan;
Then as many as could
Laid hands on the Captain
And dragged him to the stones
And thereon laid his head,
Being ready with their clubs to beat out his brains.

Pocahontas, the King's dearest daughter,
When no intreaty could prevail,
Got his head in her arms,
And laid her own upon his to save him from death.

Whereat the Emperor was contented
He should live to make him hatchets,
And her, bells, beads, and copper.

2. *Savage Entertainment*

Suddenly among the woods was heard
Such a hideous noise and shrieking
That the English betook them to their arms
Supposing Powhatan with all his power
Was come to surprise them.

But presently Pocahontas came,
Willing them to kill her

If any hurt was intended.
Then they were presented with this antic.

Thirty young women came naked out of the woods,
Covered only before and behind
With a few green leaves,
Their bodies all painted, but differing.
Their leader had buck's horns on her head,
An otter's skin at her girdle,
Another at her arm,
A quiver of arrows at her back,
A bow and arrows in her hand.
The next had in her hands a sword,
Another a club,
Another a pot-stick—
All horned alike,
The rest with their several devices.

These fiends with most hellish sounds and cries
Rushing from among the trees,
Cast themselves in a ring about the fire,
Singing and dancing with most excellent
Ill variety,
Or falling into their infernal passions,
And solemnly again to sing and dance.
And as they entered, in like manner departed.

Having reaccomodated themselves,
They invited him to their lodgings,
Where he was no sooner in the house
But all these nymphs
More tormented him than ever

With crowding, pressing, and hanging about him,
Crying, "Love you not me?
Love you not me?"

This salutation ended, the feast was set,
Consisting of all the savage dainties,
Some attending, others singing and dancing.

Which mirth being ended,
With fire-brands for torches
They conducted him to his lodging.

3. *A Dialogue of Peace and War*

The subtle savage, Powhatan,
Said, "Many do inform me,
Your coming hither is not for trade,
But to invade my people and possess my country.
To free us of this fear
Leave aboard your weapons.

"I know the difference of peace and war,
But now I am old and ere long must die.
What will it avail you to take by force
What you may quickly have by love?
Think you, I am so simple
Not to know it is better
To eat good meat,
Lie well, and sleep quietly,
Laugh and be merry with you,
Have copper, hatchets, or what I want,
Than to be forced to fly from all,

To lie cold in the woods,
Feed upon acorns, roots, and other trash,
And be so hunted by you
That I can neither rest, eat, nor sleep,
But my tired men must watch,
And if a twig break, everyone crieth
'There commeth Captain Smith!'

"And thus with miserable fear
End my miserable life,
Leaving my pleasures to such youths as you,
Which through your rashness
May quickly as miserably end.

"Let this therefore assure you of our loves,
And every year our friendly trade
Shall furnish you with corn.
Then come not thus with your guns and swords
As to invade your foes."

The Captain answered,
"Every day your promise is violated
By some of your subjects.
For your sake only we have curbed
Our thirsting desire of revenge.
As for danger from our enemies,
In such is our chief pleasure.
For your riches we have no use.
And if you should fly to the woods,
We shall not starve, as you conclude,
For we have means to find beyond your knowledge."

The King breathed his mind once more.
"None doth deny to lie at my feet,
Or refuse to do what I desire,
But only you.
If you intend so friendly as you say,
Send hence your arms."

The Captain said,
"Tomorrow I will leave my arms
And trust to your promise."

4. *Pocahontas Reveals a Plot*

Pocahontas, his dearest jewel,
In that dark night came through the irksome woods,
And told our Captain
Great cheer should be sent us by and by,
And when we were at supper
They that brought it would kill us all
With our own weapons.
But if that plot should fail,
Powhatan and all his power
Would after come to kill us.

Such things as she delighted in
He would have given her,
But with the tears running down her cheeks
She said she dared not be seen to have them,
For if Powhatan knew, she were but dead.
And so she ran away by herself as she came.

Within less than an hour
Came eight or ten lusty fellows
With platters of venison and other victual,
Very importunate to have us
Put out our matches
Whose smoke, they said, made them sick.

But the Captain made them taste every dish,
Which done he sent them back to Powhatan
To bid him make haste
For he was prepared for his coming.

5. *She Is Betrayed and Captured*

Captain Argall
Had promised Japazaws and his wife
A copper kettle
To bring her to him,
Promising no way to hurt her,
But keep her till they could conclude
A peace with her father.

And thus they betrayed the poor innocent
Pocahontas aboard,
Where they were kindly feasted in the cabin,
Japazaws treading oft on the Captain's foot
To remember he had done his part.

Then Argall told her she must go with him
And compound peace between her country and us
Before she ever should see Powhatan.
Whereat the Judas, Japazaws, and his wife

Began to howl and cry
As fast as Pocahontas.

Upon the Captain's fair persuasions
Pacifying her by degree,
Japazaws and his wife
With the kettle and other toys
Went merrily on shore.

6. *Her Wedding*

Master John Rolfe, an honest gentleman,
Had been in love with Pocahontas,
And she with him.

Which thing when I made known
By letter to Sir Thomas Dale,
He well approved.
And the bruit of this marriage coming to Powhatan,
It was acceptable to him,
As appeared by his sudden consent.
For within ten days
He sent Opachisco, her uncle, and two of his sons,
To see the manner of this marriage,
Which was about the first of April.

And ever since we have had
Friendly trade and commerce
As well with Powhatan himself
As all his subjects.

The true affection she bore for her husband,
And the strange apparitions and violent passions

He endured for her love, as he deeply protested,
Were wonderful.
And she openly renounced idolatry,
Confessed the faith of Christ,
And was baptised.

7. *Powhatan Laughs*

The first thing the King did,
He offered me a pipe of tobacco.
Then asked me how his brother
Sir Thomas Dale did, and his daughter
And unknown son,
And how they lived, loved and liked.

I told him his brother was well,
And his daughter so contented
She would not live again with him;
Whereat he laughed.

8. *A Dream in the Woods of Virginia*

I dreamed that in a wood,
Clasped as in silver when the moon
Shone clear, a woman stood.

Lady with horns,
And bow and arrows, and an otter skin,
Singing "Love you not me?"—I love you not.

Give up your naked ways,
Except a few green leaves,
Your cunning ambush where the coney plays.

Put on a skirt and hood.
Marry perhaps an English gentleman.
Though never English, you may still be good.

When I set out on my journey
It was high summer,
But now it was cold and snow lay on the ground.

I came to the great hall
Where Powhatan was sitting, with his braves
Beneath him in two rows along the wall.

I spoke. They seemed to hear.
They did not speak or move.
Then suddenly they shouted

And a wind
Rushed through the hall, the torches guttered out,
And the night was filled with sound.

IV

Whatever it is, it must have
A stomach that can digest
Rubber, coal, uranium, moons, poems.

Like the shark, it contains a shoe.
It must swim for miles through the desert
Uttering cries that are almost human.

When they had won the war
And for the first time in history
Americans were the most important people—

When the leading citizens no longer lived in
    their shirt sleeves,
And their wives did not scratch in public;
Just when they'd stopped saying "Gosh!"—

When their daughters seemed as sensitive
As the tip of a fly rod,
And their sons were as smooth as a V–8 engine—

Priests, examining the entrails of birds,
Found the heart misplaced, and seeds
As black as death, emitting a strange odor.

NIGHT FLOWERS

Leaves, what are you?

                  Flowers feed on me.

On a hill in Rome
There's my "Magnificent" with the red
Petals and white spike. In Tuscany
My "Passion." And in Paris
The orchid, blue, called by the inhabitants
"The Gendarme." I recall
The night I watered it with tears
In a room that smelled like humus.

And the cactus flowers of Monaco
On the violet-colored hill are unfolding
Near three nuns in their enormous hats
Poised on a rock like gulls or ships that sail
To Africa.

ON THE LAWN AT THE VILLA

On the lawn at the villa—
That's the way to start, eh, reader?
We know where we stand—somewhere expensive—
You and I *imperturbes,* as Walt would say,
Before the diversions of wealth, you and I *engagés.*

On the lawn at the villa
Sat a manufacturer of explosives,
His wife from Paris,
And a young man named Bruno,

And myself, being American,
Willing to talk to these malefactors,
The manufacturer of explosives, and so on,
But somehow superior. By that I mean democratic.
It's complicated, being an American,
Having the money and the bad conscience, both at
    the same time.
Perhaps, after all, this is not the right subject
    for a poem.

We were all sitting there paralyzed
In the hot Tuscan afternoon,
And the bodies of the machine-gun crew were draped
    over the balcony.
So we sat there all afternoon.

One morning, as we travelled in the fields
    Of air and dew
With trumpets, and above the painted shields
    The banners flew,

We came upon three ladies, wreathed in roses,
    Where, hand in hand,
They danced—three slender, gentle, naked ladies,
    All in a woodland.

They'd been to the best schools in Italy;
    Their legs were Greek,
Their collarbones, as fine as jewelry,
    Their eyes, antique.

"Why do lambs skip and shepherds shout 'Ut hoy!'?
    Why do you dance?"
Said one, "It is an intellectual joy,
    The Renaissance.

"As do the stars in heaven, ruled by Three,
    We twine and move.
It is the music of Astronomy,
    Not men, we love.

"And as we dance, the beasts and flowers do;
    The fields of wheat
Sway like our arms; the curving hills continue
    The curves of our feet.

"Here Raphael comes to paint; the thrushes flute
    To Petrarch's pen.
But Michael is not here, who carved the brute
    Unfinished men."

They danced again, and on the mountain heights
    There seemed to rise
Towers and ramparts glittering with lights,
    Like Paradise.

How the bright morning passed, I cannot say.
    We woke and found
The dancers gone; and heard, far, far away
    The trumpet sound.

We galloped to it. In the forest then
    Banners and shields
Were strewn like leaves; and there were many slain
    In the dark fields.

A FARM IN MINNESOTA

The corn rows walk the earth,
crowding like mankind between the fences,
feeding on sun and rain;
are broken down by hail,
or perish of incalculable drought.

And we who tend them
from the ground up—lieutenants
of this foot cavalry, leaning on fences
to watch our green men never move an inch—
who cares for us?

Our beds are sold at auction.
The Bible, and a sword—these are bequeathed
to children who prefer a modern house.
Our flesh has been consumed
only to make more lives.

But when our heads are planted
under the church, from those empty pods
we rise in the fields of death,
and are gathered by angels,
and shine in the hands of God.

LOVE, MY MACHINE

Love, my machine,
We rise by this escape,
We travel on the shocks we make.

For every man and woman
Is an immortal spirit
Trapped and dazed on a star shoot.

Tokyo, come in!
Yuzuru Karagiri, do you read me?
San Francisco, darkest of cities, do you read me?

Here is eternal space,
Here is eternal solitude.
Is it any different with you on earth?

There are so many here!
Here's Gandhi, here's Jesus,
Moses, and all the other practical people.

By the light of the stars
This night is serious.
I am going into the night to find a world of my own.

WIND, CLOUDS, AND THE
DELICATE CURVE OF THE WORLD

Wind, clouds, and the delicate curve of the world
Stretching so far away. . . .
On a cloud in the clear sight of heaven
Sit Kali and Jesus, disputing.
Tree shadows, cloud shadows
Falling across the body of the world
That sleeps with one arm thrown across her eyes. . . .
A wind stirs in the daisies
And trees are sighing,
"These houses and these gardens are illusions."
Leaf shadows, cloud shadows,
And the wind moving as far as the eye can reach. . . .

WALT WHITMAN AT BEAR MOUNTAIN

"... life which does not give the preference to any other life, of any
previous period, which therefore prefers its own existence..."
— ORTEGA Y GASSET

Neither on horseback nor seated,
But like himself, squarely on two feet,
The poet of death and lilacs
Loafs by the footpath. Even the bronze looks alive
Where it is folded like cloth. And he seems friendly.

"Where is the Mississippi panorama
And the girl who played the piano?
Where are you, Walt?
The Open Road goes to the used-car lot.

"Where is the nation you promised?
These houses built of wood sustain
Colossal snows,
And the light above the street is sick to death.

"As for the people—see how they neglect you!
Only a poet pauses to read the inscription."

"I am here," he answered.
"It seems you have found me out.
Yet, did I not warn you that it was Myself
I advertised? Were my words not sufficiently plain?

"I gave no prescriptions,
And those who have taken my moods for prophecies
Mistake the matter."
Then, vastly amused—"Why do you reproach me?

I freely confess I am wholly disreputable.
Yet I am happy, because you have found me out."

A crocodile in wrinkled metal loafing ...

Then all the realtors,
Pickpockets, salesmen, and the actors performing
Official scenarios,
Turned a deaf ear, for they had contracted
American dreams.

But the man who keeps a store on a lonely road,
And the housewife who knows she's dumb,
And the earth, are relieved.

All that grave weight of America
Cancelled! Like Greece and Rome.
The future in ruins!
The castles, the prisons, the cathedrals
Unbuilding, and roses
Blossoming from the stones that are not there. . . .

The clouds are lifting from the high Sierras,
The Bay mists clearing.
And the angel in the gate, the flowering plum,
Dances like Italy, imagining red.

PACIFIC IDEAS—A LETTER TO WALT WHITMAN

When the schooners were drifting
Over the hills—schooners like white skulls—
The sun was the clock in that parlor
And the piano was played by the wind.

But a man must sit down,
And things, after all, are necessary.
Those "immensely overpaid accounts,"
Walt, it seems that we must pay them again.

It's hard to civilize, to change
The usual order;
And the young, who are always the same, endlessly
Rehearse the fate of Achilles.

Everyone wants to live at the center,
"The world of the upper floors."
And the sad professors of English
Are wishing that they were dead, as usual.

But here is the sea and the mist,
Gray Lethe of forgetfulness,
And the moon, gliding from the mist,
Love, with her garland of dreams.

And I have quarrelled with my books
For the moon is not in their fable,
And say to darkness, Let your dragon come,
O anything, to hold her in my arms!

LINES WRITTEN NEAR SAN FRANCISCO

I wake and feel the city trembling.
Yes, there is something unsettled in the air
And the earth is uncertain.

And so it was for the tenor Caruso.
He couldn't sleep—you know how the ovation
Rings in your ears, and you re-sing your part.

And then the ceiling trembled
And the floor moved. He ran into the street.
Never had Naples given him such a reception!

The air was darker than Vesuvius.
"O mamma mia,"
He cried, "I've lost my voice!"

At that moment the hideous voice of Culture,
Hysterical woman, thrashing her arms and legs,
Shrieked from the ruins.

At that moment everyone became a performer.
Otello and Don Giovanni
And Figaro strode on the midmost stage.

In the high window of a burning castle
Lucia raved. Black horses
Plunged through fire, dragging the wild bells.

The curtains were wrapped in smoke. Tin swords
Were melting; masks and ruffs
Burned—and the costumes of the peasants' chorus.

Night fell. The white moon rose
And sank in the Pacific. The tremors
Passed under the waves. And Death rested.

2

Now, as we stand idle,
Watching the silent, bowler-hatted man,
The engineer, who writes in the smoking field;

Now as he hands the paper to a boy,
Who takes it and runs to a group of waiting men,
And they disperse and move toward their wagons,

Mules bray and the wagons move—
Wait! Before you start
(Already the wheels are rattling on the stones)

Say, did your fathers cross the dry Sierras
To build another London?
Do Americans always have to be second-rate?

Wait! For there are spirits
In the earth itself, or the air, or sea.
Where are the aboriginal American devils?

Cloud shadows, pine shadows
Falling across the bright Pacific bay . . .
(Already they have nailed rough boards together)

Wait only for the wind
That rustles in the eucalyptus tree.
Wait only for the light

That trembles on the petals of a rose.
(The mortar sets—banks are the first to stand)
Wait for a rose, and you may wait forever.

The silent man mops his head and drinks
Cold lemonade. "San Francisco
Is a city second only to Paris."

3

Every night, at the end of America
We taste our wine, looking at the Pacific.
How sad it is, the end of America!

While we were waiting for the land
They'd finished it—with gas drums
On the hilltops, cheap housing in the valleys

Where lives are mean and wretched.
But the banks thrive and the realtors
Rejoice—they have their America.

Still, there is something unsettled in the air.
Out there on the Pacific
There's no America but the Marines.

Whitman was wrong about the People,
But right about himself. The land is within.
At the end of the open road we come to ourselves.

Though mad Columbus follows the sun
Into the sea, we cannot follow.
We must remain, to serve the returning sun,

And to set tables for death.
For we are the colonists of Death—
Not, as some think, of the English.

And we are preparing thrones for him to sit,
Poems to read, and beds
In which it may please him to rest.

This is the land
The pioneers looked for, shading their eyes
Against the sun—a murmur of serious life.

THE WESLEYAN POETRY PROGRAM

*Distinguished books of contemporary poetry
available in cloth-bound and paperback editions
published by Wesleyan University Press*

Alan Ansen:	*Disorderly Houses* (1961)
John Ashbery:	*The Tennis Court Oath* (1962)
Robert Bagg:	*Madonna of the Cello* (1961)
Robert Bly:	*Silence in the Snowy Fields* (1962)
Donald Davie:	*New and Selected Poems* (1961)
James Dickey:	*Drowning With Others* (1962)
David Ferry:	*On the Way to the Island* (1960)
Robert Francis:	*The Orb Weaver* (1960)
Richard Howard:	*Quantities* (1962)
Barbara Howes:	*Light and Dark* (1959)
David Ignatow:	*Say Pardon* (1961)
Donald Justice:	*The Summer Anniversaries* (1960) (A Lamont Poetry Selection)
Chester Kallman:	*Absent and Present* (1963)
Vassar Miller:	*My Bones Being Wiser* (1963)
Vassar Miller:	*Wage War on Silence* (1960)
Hyam Plutzik:	*Apples from Shinar* (1959)
Louis Simpson:	*At the End of the Open Road* (1963)
Louis Simpson:	*A Dream of Governors* (1959)
James Wright:	*The Branch Will Not Break* (1963)
James Wright:	*Saint Judas* (1959)